TUBU:
The Teda
and the
Daza

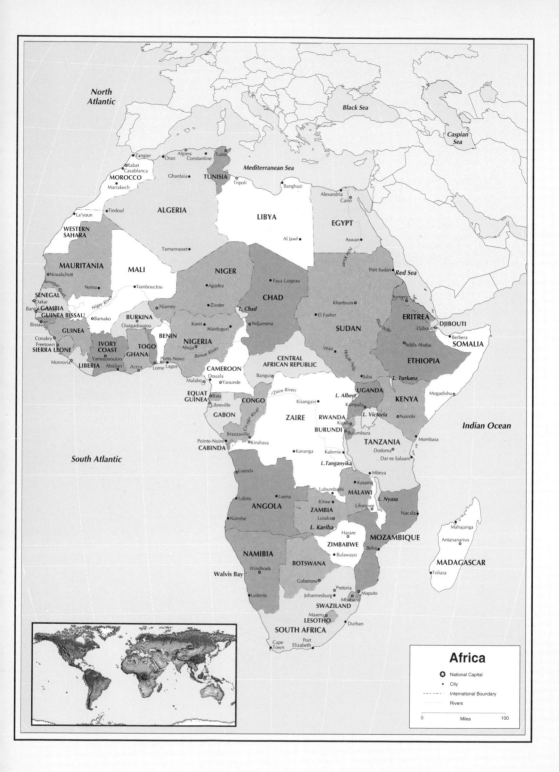

Africa

⊛ National Capital
• City
- - - International Boundary
~~~ Rivers

0　　　　Miles　　　100

TUBU: The Teda and the Daza

Catherine Baroin, Ph.D.

THE ROSEN PUBLISHING GROUP, INC.
NEW YORK

Published in 1997 by The Rosen Publishing Group, Inc.
29 East 21st Street, New York, NY 10010

First Edition

Manufactured in the United States of America

Library of Congress Cataloging-in-Publication Data

Baroin, Catherine.
    Tubu : the Teda and the Daza / Catherine Baroin. — 1st ed.
      p.   cm. — (The heritage library of African peoples)
    Includes bibliographical references and index.
    Summary: Surveys the culture, history, and contemporary life of
these two groups in the Sahara desert and in the Sahel regions of Chad.
    ISBN 0-8239-2000-3
    1. Teda (African people)—History—Juvenile literature. 2. Teda
(African people)—Social life and customs—Juvenile literature.
3. Daza (African people)—History—Juvenile literature. 4. Daza
(African people)—Social life and customs—Juvenile literature.
[1. Teda (African people) 2. Daza (African people)] I. Title.
II. Series.
DT546.445.T4B37   1996
967.43—dc20   96-32802
                                                         CIP
                                                         AC

Contents

INTRODUCTION

THERE IS EVERY REASON FOR US TO KNOW something about Africa and to understand its past and the way of life of its peoples. Africa is a rich continent that has for centuries provided the world with art, culture, labor, wealth, and natural resources. It has vast mineral deposits, fossil fuels, and commercial crops.

But perhaps most important is the fact that fossil evidence indicates that human beings originated in Africa. The earliest traces of human beings and their tools are almost two million years old. Their descendants have migrated throughout the world. To be human is to be of African descent.

The experiences of the peoples who stayed in Africa are as rich and as diverse as of those who established themselves elsewhere. This series of books describes their environment, their modes of subsistence, their relationships, and their customs and beliefs. The books present the variety of languages, histories, cultures, and religions that are to be found on the African continent. They demonstrate the historical linkages between African peoples and the way contemporary Africa has been affected by European colonial rule.

Africa is large, complex, and diverse. It encompasses an area of more than 11,700,000

square miles. The United States, Europe, and India could fit easily into it. The sheer size is an indication of the continent's great variety in geography, terrain, climate, flora, fauna, peoples, languages, and cultures.

Much of contemporary Africa has been shaped by European colonial rule, industrialization, urbanization, and the demands of a world economic system. For more than seventy years, large regions of Africa were ruled by Great Britain, France, Belgium, Portugal, and Spain. African peoples from various ethnic, linguistic, and cultural backgrounds were brought together to form colonial states.

For decades Africans struggled to gain their independence. It was not until after World War II that the colonial territories became independent African states. Today, almost all of Africa is ruled by Africans. Large numbers of Africans live in modern cities. Rural Africa is also being transformed, and yet its people still engage in many of their customs and beliefs.

Contemporary circumstances and natural events have not always been kind to ordinary Africans. Today, however, new popular social movements and technological innovations pose great promise for future development.

George C. Bond, Ph.D., Director
Institute of African Studies
Columbia University, New York

The Tubu live in harsh environments. They must make the most of the resources that are available to them. Date palms (above) are a very important source of food for those Tubu who live in the oases of the Borkou region of Chad.

chapter

1

THE LAND AND
THE PEOPLE

THE TUBU ARE SOMETIMES CALLED THE "black nomads of the Sahara." They are an important group of herders living in the Sahara Desert and the Sahel region, which makes up the southern fringe of the Sahara. The area where they live is extremely large. It spans over 750 miles from north to south, and even more from east to west, covering about one fourth of the Sahara, and spreading into four different countries: Chad, Niger, Libya, and Sudan (*see map*). Most Tubu, however, live north of Lake Chad in northern Chad. This area is called the Chadian Desert. It is made up of the parts of the Sahara and Sahel that are located in modern-day Chad.

The few people who live in the Sahara Desert itself are settled in big oases where date palms are grown, such as the oases of Borkou, 375

9

miles north of Lake Chad. Most of the population lives in the Sahel zone.

Due to the small amount of rain that falls in July and August, the Sahel region has a few thorny trees and some grass that dries up quickly after the rainy season. Because rainfall is scarce and unreliable, farming is possible only in a few irrigated areas and people must rely on herding for their living. They breed camels, sheep, and goats. In fact, the Tubu's camels are the one-humped kind that are more accurately called dromedaries.

Tubu living close to the Sahelian pastures in the south also breed cattle. However, in the past severe droughts have killed many cattle. This led many herders to replace their cattle with camels, which resist drought better. Even in good years when rainfall is plentiful, herders must move their animals from pasture to pasture all year round. Because they have no fixed homes, most Tubu lead a nomadic life.

In the far north of the Chadian Desert is a vast area of highlands called Tibesti, which reaches a height of 10,000 feet. Summer rainfall is not always plentiful, but the cool highland climate allows some pastures to grow. The pastures feed a few goats and camels. In the local language, Tibesti is called *Tu*. This is how the people who lived there got their name *Tubu*, which means the people of Tu. Because of the

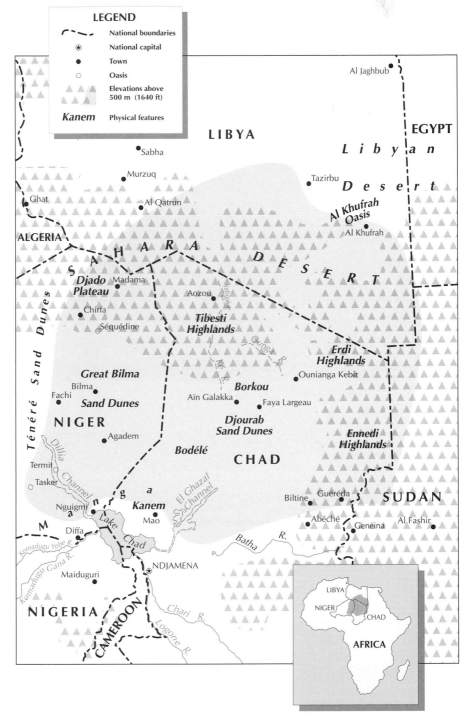

The Tubu are found mainly in Chad. In northern Chad they call themselves the Teda. The Teda live in the Sahara Desert on the Tibesti Highlands and in the oases of the Borkou region. They keep camels and goats. The Tubu in southern Chad call themselves the Daza. They occupy the Sahel region south of the Sahara. Here there is enough grass to keep cattle.

The Sahel region in southern Chad (above) has scattered vegetation and grazing for cattle. Northern Chad is part of the Sahara Desert and is so dry that cattle cannot survive. The Tubu who live in this area keep camels (below.)

very harsh conditions of life in Tibesti today, it is very sparsely populated. Because of both the height and the climate access to the Tibesti highlands is difficult. Their landscape has protected the Tubu in times of war.

To the outside world, the peoples of northern Chad are known as Tubu. However, the people themselves do not use this name. In the north they call themselves Teda (singular: Tede) and in the south, Daza (singular: Daze). The Teda and Daza societies are basically the same, and the Teda and Daza can be considered one people.

The main difference between them is that they live in separate areas: the Teda are desert people who breed camels and small livestock, while the Daza in the Sahel also breed cattle. They also speak different dialects: the Teda speak *teda-ga*, which means the language of the Teda, and the Daza speak *daza-ga*, the language of the Daza. However, these two dialects are considered to be one language. It is similar to Kanuri, which is spoken in Bornu in northern Nigeria.▲

chapter

2

HISTORY AND RELIGION

IN PREHISTORIC TIMES THE SAHARA DESERT was a wet and green area where many animals lived, including hippopotamuses, giraffes, and elephants. Images of these animals were painted on rocks by the people who lived there. Their paintings can still be seen in many areas of the Chadian Desert. The people who painted these images have long since disappeared. There is no evidence to suggest that these ancient cave painters were the ancestors of the Tubu.

▼ ANCIENT HISTORY ▼

Our knowledge of the Tubu's ancient history is very poor because no historical documents remain to describe the past. Herodotus, a Greek historian from 400 BC, is the first writer to mention that there were people living in the Chadian Desert. Much later two Arab geographers, Idrisi

in the 1100s and Leo Africanus in the 1500s, also wrote about these people. Unfortunately, their descriptions are vague. It is not clear whether the people they describe were the ancestors of the present-day Tubu or some other previous inhabitants of the area. Whatever the case may be, the Tubu have certainly lived in the region for a very long time.

▼ RECENT PAST ▼

Little is known about the ancient history of the Tubu. But their more recent history—from the 1700s onward—is recorded in written documents and oral histories, which have been passed from generation to generation by word of mouth. Each Tubu group has its own oral histories.

However, only the old men in Tubu society know their traditions well. Few young people today care about them. Because there are so many Tubu groups, it is difficult to collect and compile all of their oral histories. These histories recount the many wars and raids against other Tubu groups and neighboring peoples.

The Tuareg, who live in the Sahara to the west of the Tubu, have been long-standing enemies of the Tubu. Besides minor raids, the main source of conflict between the Tubu and other groups was control of the salt caravan. Each year the Tuareg set out with several thousand camels from the Aïr Mountains in Niger. They traveled several hundred miles east to Bilma to get mineral salt for trade, for personal use, and for the health of their camels. From the 1700s until the beginning of the twentieth century, the Tubu often raided this yearly caravan.

At the end of the 1700s, the Turks ruled the region north of Tubu country called Fezzan, which lies in the south of modern-day Libya. From there, the Turks sent different Arab groups to fight the Tubu. But the Tubu's most dangerous enemies at the end of the 1800s were the Ulad Sulayman Arabs. After they were defeated by the Turks, this Arab group invaded all of Tubu country. In addition to swords and spears, which most Tubu carried at that time, the Arabs also had rifles. Firearms gave the Arabs great advantage over the Tubu.

Like the Tubu, the Tuareg and Arabs were nomads and warriors, and they shared a similar way of life. Theirs was a very different lifestyle than that of the farmers who were growing millet on the southern fringes of the Sahara. These farmers were often raided by their nomadic northern neighbors.

Because they lived on the outskirts of the desert, the Tubu were also regular targets for raiding nomads from farther north. As a result, the Tubu and the millet farmers became allies. The farmers gave part of their harvest and other

goods to the Tubu nomads in exchange for their protection from other raiders.

▼ COLONIZATION ▼

Precolonial Tubu society was composed of many different groups, each of a different size. These groups fought frequently and changed alliances with one another. Each group had its own leader, but each leader had very little influence over the other members of his group, except when leading raids. Individualism was, and still is, an important idea among the Tubu. Tubu men in general believe that there is no one they should obey but themselves.

These factors made it very difficult for the French to conquer the Tubu and control them. The French took control of the Lake Chad area in 1900. They conquered Tibesti in 1914, but they left the area soon afterward because of World War I. The French resumed their occupation of Tibesti in 1929.

French control reduced the disputes and the raiding of animals between different Tubu groups. This promoted peace in the region. The population grew and the economic situation of most people improved.

However, the French presence, while good in some ways, deeply changed the traditional Tubu way of life. The traditional role of the Tubu leader was completely undermined. Instead of leading raids, Tubu chiefs became figureheads. They were required to convey orders and collect taxes for the French. If a Tubu leader refused to cooperate, the French colonizers would choose a new chief to replace him. This caused a great deal of resentment among the Tubu.

The colonial period was relatively peaceful. However, like other African peoples, the Tubu and their neighbors wanted to be free of the colonizers. Chad became independent in 1960. A few years later, a civil war broke out in northern Chad that lasted for twenty years.

▼ RELIGION ▼

Today all Tubu are Muslims. Because the introduction of Islam was a very slow and irregular process, a precise date for its introduction is difficult to give. The religion spread to the different Tubu social groups at different speeds and times. It generally reached men before women. This process took many years throughout the 1800s.

Today people living in the Sahara and Sahel, from Mauritania to Sudan and Egypt, are almost all Muslims. This includes all the Tubu's neighbors—the Tuareg to the west, the Fulani to the east, and the different Arab tribes to the north in Libya and to the south and east in Chad and Sudan.

The Tubu are Muslims, meaning they follow the religion of Islam. Muslims are required to offer daily prayers. During prayer they must face the holy city of Mecca in Saudi Arabia and touch their foreheads to the ground (top). Women sit apart from men during Muslim ceremonies, usually behind the men (bottom).

These peoples do not speak the same language. Each one has a distinct culture. Although the Tubu say their prayers in Arabic, few Tubu actually speak Arabic. For the most part, they know only a few Arabic words used in trade.

19

The Tubu follow Islam by obeying the Muslim rules of saying daily prayers, observing the annual Ramadan fast, and making a pilgrimage to Mecca by the few who can afford it. In addition, they also practice Islamic customs such as the circumcision of boys, the dowry given to a bride, and Muslim rules concerning inheritance and burial ceremonies.

Before Islam arrived, the Tubu practiced a traditional religion that included ancestor worship and ceremonies to promote rain. Little is left of this religion today. However, apart from these important changes in religion, the Teda and Daza have retained much of their own culture and many of their social rules.▲

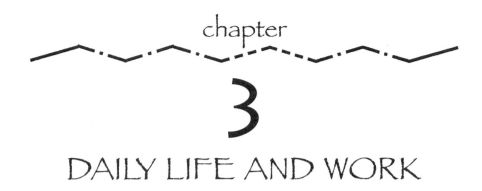

chapter

3

DAILY LIFE AND WORK

THE DAILY LIFE OF TUBU FAMILIES IN different regions can vary greatly. The cattle breeders in the Sahel, the desert dwellers in the Sahara, and the families that eat date palms and farm irrigated fields in the Borkou oases all have distinct lifestyles. However different their daily activities, all Tubu people share a common culture.

Tubu society, like many others in the world, is separated into two different worlds: masculine and feminine, each with very different activities.

A Tubu woman takes care of her young children and the family tent (or house, in a settled environment), which belongs to her. She keeps the tent tidy, makes sure it is supplied with firewood and water, and prepares the meals. She also takes care of young animals, which are kept near the home until they are weaned. She milks both the cattle and the camels, but churns only

THE ETIQUETTE OF MEALS

Meals for the whole family are prepared by the mother or one of her older daughters. However, Tubu etiquette allows only certain family members to eat together.

The father eats with other adult men, including neighbors and guests. They eat from a common bowl. His sons are not allowed to share his meal before they become full adults, that is, not before they are about thirty years old. Daughters eat with their mothers from a young age. There is more intimacy and less formality between them than between a father and his sons.

Husband and wife, and men and women in general, never eat together: this is strictly prohibited. A husband never eats in the presence of his wife, although a wife may eat when her husband is around. However, after about three years of marriage, a married couple may start drinking tea together. For the wife, tea drinking is a relatively new habit. Young girls are not allowed to drink tea. Only after marriage may they begin to drink tea with other people of similar age.

These strict rules that separate the sexes during meals do not apply to young children. Brothers and sisters may eat together when they are young, before puberty. Similarly, a very old woman may share her meal with a small boy.

The Tubu prefer to eat discreetly. They avoid strong light at the evening meal. The kerosene light is put aside in a corner of the room. People usually eat silently. It is a mistake to start saying something that comes to mind while eating. When the common bowl is nearly empty, people politely begin to stop eating and lick their fingers carefully, leaving one person to finish the dish.

One of the main tasks of Tubu women in the Sahel is milking the cows (above).

the cows' milk. Watering the herds from the well is a strenuous task that is performed by men, women, and teenagers.

Men's duties include looking after the herds, searching for stray animals, and pursuing thieves. Grazing cattle stay together and never stray far from the camp. But camels tend to scatter and cover much greater distances. Looking after camels thus requires long days of walking in the bush or desert, good knowledge of the

Most of Tubu men's time is spent tending their herds. Seen above are animals drinking from a well in the Sahel. The watering hole has been covered with branches to prevent the animals from stepping in it. Seen below is a camel market near Lake Chad.

country, and the ability to recognize and track every animal from its footprints on the sand. The art of tracking animals takes many years of practice to master.

A man is also responsible for providing food for his family. Together with milk and dates, millet forms the basis of the Teda and Daza diet. A Teda or Daza man must often travel several days to buy millet at a market. Once there, he sells a few animals to get enough money to stock up on millet, tea, and sugar for his family. Strong, sweet tea is the favorite drink of the Teda and Daza and is sometimes drunk in place of food if none is available. Occasionally, a Teda or Daza man will also buy clothes, shoes, perfume, enameled bowls, or other household utensils to take home.

A man also makes frequent visits to his relatives and in-laws in neighboring camps. Women travel also, mainly to visit their relatives. But they can only leave their tents or houses when they have somebody else to milk the animals and take care of their small children. A woman must have an older daughter, a willing neighbor, or a female relative to do her work while she is away. This means that a woman never travels as far or as often as her husband does.

▼ **HAIRSTYLES AND CLOTHING** ▼
According to Muslim tradition, a baby is

Tubu men generally wear turbans like these (above) worn by young Daza men from eastern Niger. Married women, like the Daza woman below, wear distinctive hairstyles that are a sign of their married status.

given a Muslim name and its head is shaved seven days after it is born. Young children, both boys and girls, keep their heads shaved for several years. They are completely bald except for a crest, a strip of hair that runs from the tip of the forehead to the nape of the neck. Depending on family habits, children also may have one or a few tufts of hair on the top and sides of their heads.

Twenty years ago, it was common for boys to go naked until they were six or seven years old. Girls wore only a small strip of cloth around their waists. Perhaps because of the growing influence of Islam, most children start wearing clothes at a much younger age today.

Boys are circumcised around thirteen years old, about the time that they reach puberty. From that point on, they are regarded as men. They usually shave their heads as they did before. Like other men, they wear wide cotton pants, long shirts, and turbans on their heads. A turban is a long piece of cotton cloth wrapped around the head, often in a stylish fashion. When traveling, a turban is worn over the nose and mouth to protect a person from the desert heat and dust.

Between the ages of ten and thirteen, girls tattoo their lower lips to make them darker and bigger. First, the lip is pricked with hard thorns from the surrounding trees. Then charcoal dust is smeared into the wounds to darken the lip. While boys keep their heads shaved at this age, girls start to let their hair grow. When it is long enough, they make small parallel braids that run from the forehead to the back of the head.

Two or three years later, girls start to wear their hair in the style of women of marriageable age. This hairdo is composed of three parallel braids that run from the forehead to the nape of the neck, with a large number of thinner braids running down on each side. All of these braids are smeared with a mixture of perfumed powder and oil or butter. Because it takes a long time to braid the entire head, girls have their hair done only once a month or so. A woman will be praised for her long hair and clear

Long hair is a sign of beauty among the Tubu. Hairstyles are smeared with perfumed powder mixed into oil or butter.

complexion. These are the two most important qualities for Tubu feminine beauty.

In the past anyone in Tubu country knew from a woman's hairdo whether or not she was married. Married women wore only two thick braids instead of three. Divorced women or widows only had one braid. Today, however, these customary hairstyles are changing fast. Tubu women are now wearing many different hairstyles. Even men are sometimes letting their hair grow long.

Today many women also prefer to wear bright robes instead of their traditional dark garments. Made from a single large piece of black or dark blue cotton cloth, the traditional garment was wrapped around a woman's waist and knotted on top of her left shoulder.

▼ CHILDREN'S DAILY ACTIVITIES ▼

Young children usually play near their mothers. The children make their own toys when they become old enough. Boys like to make cars with old cans, sticks of wood, and a bit of rope.

As they grow up, Tubu boys and girls start to help with the family chores. The jobs are divided among the children according to their sex and age. Little by little, boys are trained in male activities and girls, in female ones.

A five-year-old boy may be asked to watch the cows at the well. He must make sure that

Tubu boys make their own toys, such as cars (left), and learn skills from their fathers, such as making rope (right).

the cows take turns, and that each gets its share of water. The boy chases away disobedient cows with a long wooden stick that may be over ten times bigger than he is!

When they are between seven and ten years old, boys learn many skills from their fathers and other men. For example, they learn how to make rope for tying animals and saddles for camels. They learn to ride these animals at a very young age.

Teenage boys learn to track lost animals. They also learn how to find their way alone in the wilderness. Before they are twenty years old, Tubu boys know how to take care of their fathers' herds. With other boys their age, they

often tend their fathers' camels on the desert pastures. The older men in Tubu society take care of social duties while their sons handle the animals.

Young girls receive a different type of education than that of the boys. As a young child, a Tubu girl follows her mother around and learns how to do household chores. At six or seven, she starts to fetch wood and water for the kitchen. She also learns how to churn milk, take care of young animals, watch her younger brothers and sisters, and keep an eye on the fire.

As soon as they are strong enough, both boys and girls help to water the cattle and camels. Because family tents are scattered far apart and schools are too far away, only a few Tubu children attend school regularly.▲

chapter

4

THE FAMILY HOUSEHOLD

THE BASIC TUBU SOCIAL UNIT IS THE family, consisting of a husband, a wife, and their children. The family usually lives in a tent made of several large mats tied onto a wooden frame.

There are, however, some exceptions to this traditional type of housing. In Tibesti, the tent is sometimes replaced with a permanent house, which is made of a low, circular stone wall covered with palm branches or reeds. In the oases of Borkou and in the valleys of Tibesti, there are some permanent villages with rectangular, flat-roofed houses made of mud. But the tent is the type of dwelling that is most suited to the Teda and Daza way of life.

The shape of the tent varies according to the season. In winter, in places where there is not too much wind, a rectangular shape is often preferred, because it is thought to retain heat better. (It can be very cold in the Sahara. Water

Tents are well-suited to the way of life of many Tubu, who must often move with their animals to find fertile grazing lands. These women are taking down a tent.

freezes at night in winter.) In May and June, before the rainy season begins, the tents in the Sahel region are given curved tops. This shape helps the tents to resist the strong winds that blow at this time of year. Later, during the rainy season, very small tents are built, using only scraps of mats. The Tubu prefer not to use their bigger, newer mats because the rains would darken and spoil them.

Because of the limited space household furniture inside the tent is minimal. Three stones or a tripod to hold the cooking pot can be found in a corner. The man's *malamala*, a big, leather travel bag decorated with long red leather strips that flap on the camel's sides when the man rides, hangs on one side of the tent. There is also a *shuwi*, which is a big, hollowed-out gourd used

33

This man in a market in northern Nigeria is making *malamala* leather bags to sell to Tubu travelers.

for churning milk, and a few bags or woven pots for storing clothes and food. A metal suitcase, locked with a padlock, is kept on the bed. Here the family keeps its most valuable belongings, such as a few pictures and papers, some money, salt, tea, and the wife's mirror and perfumes. The bed itself is made of a wide mat stretched over short pegs. The pegs stand about four inches above the ground and are used to avoid snakes and scorpions. The family tent and furniture can all be tied onto the back of one camel when it is time to move.

A family tent seldom stands alone; similar tents are scattered nearby, making a small camp. Not far away is the well, where the herds are watered, one after the other, from morning till night. The women also come here to get water for cooking and drinking. Some wells are

cemented, but others are still lined with logs of wood to prevent the sand from falling in, and they do not last very long. It is a specialist's job to dig and line a new well.

Each Tubu family is independent and decides where to settle, but men usually prefer to live near their brothers. Most of them have only one wife, because Tubu women make life difficult for their husbands if they decide to take a second wife. Nonetheless, a few rich men have two wives, but their wives live in different places in order to avoid quarrels.▲

chapter

5

MARRIAGE

MOST TUBU GIRLS MARRY BETWEEN FIFTEEN and twenty years of age. Men marry much later, usually between twenty-five and thirty.

It is a disgrace for a Teda or Daza to marry a close relative, such as a cousin, although this is the preferred type of marriage in the Arab world. A Tubu marriage is forbidden if the two partners have a common grandparent, great-grandparent, or even a great-great-grandparent.

When an agreement has been reached between two families for their son and daughter to marry, many payments must be made by the groom's family to the bride's before the wedding can take place. The payment process often takes at least two years. But all these payments, and even more, are returned by the wife's family to the bridegroom on the wedding day or some years later.

A Tubu wedding ceremony takes place in the

girl's camp, where a brand-new tent is built early in the morning, not far from that of the bride's parents. In the late afternoon, small groups of guests begin to arrive from all directions. Some travel on camel or horseback, others by foot. Three hundred people or more may gather for the event.

As the guests arrive drums are beaten and young men and girls dance in a circle, swaying their necks and bodies discreetly. These Tubu dances, which are very sober and elegant, last until late at night. A lot of food (millet and meat) and sweet tea is prepared for the wedding guests.

Following Tubu customs, the bride and the bridegroom do not take part in these festivities.

In the evening, the bridegroom is brought to the wedding tent. He rides a camel or a horse, and a young boy sits behind him in order to bring him good luck.

Later the men from the bride's and groom's families gather for the Muslim part of the ceremony. They make sure that the dowry has been given by the bridegroom's parents to the bride. This is a gift that the woman will keep for herself if ever her husband rejects her. Once the dowry transfer is settled, the men all pray together.

On the second day, more food is prepared for the guests who have spent the night in different

On the day of his wedding a Tubu groom is brought to the wedding tent. He rides a horse or camel, and a young boy is seated behind him for luck (above).

tents in the camp. The drum is beaten and the young people begin to dance again. Camel races are also organized. These events give young men the opportunity to impress the young women watching them with their riding skills. The bridegroom, meanwhile, remains in his tent, silently watching from a distance.

In the afternoon, the animals given to the bridegroom by the bride's family are brought together for all to see. This is a very cheerful time. The herd that has just been given to the young man will now enable him to lead an independent life.

It is only after sunset on the second day that the bride is brought to the wedding tent. An older woman takes her by force out of the tent

THE TUBU BRIDE

A young Daza or Teda girl is expected to remain a virgin until she is ready to be married, between the ages of fifteen and twenty. Her parents take charge of finding a husband for her. They accept or reject marriage proposals as they see fit. Usually the girl herself has no say in the matter. Sometimes she does not even know to whom she is being married until the day of the wedding. If she does know who her fiancé is, it is highly improper for her to talk about him to others.

After the wedding, however, she shows her feelings by the way she behaves. For many days or even months after the wedding, the newlyweds' tent is set up inside the bride's parents' camp. She knows all her neighbors well. It is customary for the bride to leave the wedding tent at night and hide in a neighbor's tent or in the bush. Her husband, left alone in the tent, has no way to make his bride return. After showing proper reluctance for some time, the wife will stop fleeing at nightfall if she approves of her husband.

If the new wife dislikes her husband, she will continue to leave the tent for many months. This is a very powerful way of showing her feelings. If she is determined enough, and many Tubu brides are remarkably so, the husband will finally give up. He will then have no option but to divorce her by saying "*Sor*," meaning "I leave (you)."

After such a divorce, the bride and her friends rejoice. From then on the former wife is a divorcée, or *ogu*. She keeps her own tent in her parents' camp and has a very free lifestyle. She eventually begins to take part in young people's dances at night. Bachelors and other *ogu* women often gather in her tent at night to party. One young man generally plays the lute while the others play cards and drink tea together. The *ogu* may choose one of these men as her lover. After a year or two she can marry someone she loves.

where she has been hiding and dresses her with new clothes. Then she wraps the bride in a rug so that nobody can see her. Several women from her family carry the bride on their heads to the wedding tent, now and then stopping and singing a special song along the way.

The ceremony is now over and the guests begin to depart. The newlywed couple, however, must stay inside their tent without leaving for the next seven days.

For the following two years or so, the young man must work for his father-in-law. This period is called *yollumi*. Young men dislike it, because they resent the lack of freedom and the strict etiquette that requires them to avoid their mothers-in-law, who live just next door. *Yollumi* ends when the father-in-law deems it appropriate. The young man is then free to set up his tent wherever he wishes, taking his wife away with him.▲

chapter

6
SOCIETY

MOST OF THE TEDA AND DAZA POPULATION is made up of Tubu clans. There is no social difference between Teda and Daza clans, and the people may marry each other. But there are three other categories of people who are not regarded as fully Tubu and whom the Tubu clans will generally not marry: smiths, slaves, and farmers.

▼ SMITHS ▼

The smiths are called *aza* (singular: *eze*) in both the Teda and Daza languages. Some *aza* are actual blacksmiths who make tools and weapons such as knives, swords, and spears. These weapons are still made and used today. No Teda or Daza man goes anywhere without his dagger, which he carries in a leather sheath tied to his left elbow. Women also carry weapons, which they use on occasion.

Many smiths, however, make their livings
from activities other than weaponry, which are
also specific to the *aza*. Some smiths specialize
in making silver or gold jewelry. Others deal in
leather crafts, making travel bags, sheaths, shoes,
and charms. Charms are small leather bags con-
taining verses of the Koran that bring the bearer
luck. All Teda and Daza wear such charms to
protect them, especially when they leave home.
Other activities of *aza* men include digging and
lining wells, and playing music in public with
special drums, called *kidi*.

Aza women lead lives similar to other Teda
and Daza women. They take care of their
houses, children,
and animals.
But they also
specialize in

Aza men may be
blacksmiths, jewelers,
or craftsmen. This
man is sharpening a
blade on his anvil.

the weaving of tent mats. They sell these mats to other Teda or Daza women for whom this task is regarded as too lowly.

Tubu society is not the only one where marrying a smith is strictly prohibited for those who are not smiths. Such is the case in many societies around the world, especially in the Sahara and Sahel.

▼ SLAVES ▼

Like the smiths, slaves were avoided as marriage partners by non-slaves. For this reason, the slaves typically did not marry outside of their social status.

In the past, the slave class was made up of mainly children raided from non-Islamic peoples living in the south of Chad or in the mountains north of Cameroon. Removed from their own families and brought up by Tubu families, these young slaves soon forgot their

Aza women specialize in making tent mats.

mother tongues. They learned the Tubu language and adapted to the Tubu culture. The slaves were given the most difficult tasks to perform.

When slavery ended, many slaves continued to live with their masters because they felt they had nowhere else to go. They did not have large or wealthy families to rely on and had no land on which to grow crops for food.

Today, the Teda and Daza are still strongly prejudiced against slaves. This is illustrated by a Teda tale about the silliness of nine slaves who pretended to go raiding like nobles (*see box*). Raiding used to be a prestigious activity in which the slaves never took part.

▼ THE *KAMAYA* ▼

A third social category is that of small farmers called *kamaya* (singular: *kamaye*). These farmers are found mainly in the north, in the Tibesti and Borkou regions. They have a mixed ancestry, which can be traced to people who lived in the region before the Tubu arrived and to slaves and outlaws. In the past, outlaws would often flee far from the scenes of their crimes and settle in a new place to escape punishment.

The status of the *kamaya* is higher than that of slaves, but below what is considered to be Teda or Daza proper. They grow food on small plots of land in the irrigated gardens of the Borkou region, or along the temporary streams

"THE SILLINESS OF SLAVES"

Nine slaves went raiding. They found ten camels and stole them. Each slave took one for himself, so there was one left. Each one said to the next, "Please take the last one!" To this, each replied, "No, my family is not any nobler than yours, so there is no reason why I should take it instead of you."

They finally decided to go to a Muslim scholar (*maallem*) to help them solve the problem.

"Well, it is quite easy," said the scholar, "One camel for nine slaves, nine camels for one scholar!"

"You are right," answered the slaves.

(*Recorded in Niger in 1971*)

This story about slaves and camels illustrates the prejudice against slaves in Tubu society.

running down the valleys of Tibesti. They enjoy more freedom than the slaves, but many of them still do not own the land they farm.

The *kamaya*, *aza*, and slaves together make up only a small part of the Tubu population.

The Tubu's animals often stray far from the herd in their search for food. Branding, as they are doing here, with special marks makes it easy to tell which clan owns a lost animal.

The main bulk is composed of the Teda or Daza proper, who are divided into clans.

▼ CLANS ▼

The Teda and Daza are divided into numerous patrilineal clans. The people trace their ancestry through the family line of the men.

Clan members share a common name and the same camel brands. These are geometrical designs that are branded with a hot iron onto the animals as a sign of property. Some brands are shared by different clans because the clans are related or allied.

In the past Teda and Daza clans migrated over long distances. They often fought one another over land and resources. They also fought against some of their neighbors, such as

SOME TEDA AND DAZA BRANDS

kwili-nga
"on the thigh"
This brand is used by the Daza
clans called Sagarda and Sulumpa.

mede-nga
"on the buttock"
This brand is used by the Daza
Moge clan.

taare
"small ax"
This brand is used by the Teda
Gunda clan.

tomal
"kettle drum"
This brand is used by the Daza
Kesherda, who received it from the
sultan of Bornu, in northern Nigeria.

domalai
"throwing knife"
This brand is used by many Teda and
Daza clans.

kurkia agozo
"three strokes"
This brand is used by the Teda Gunda
and the Daza Tommulia.

the Tuareg or Arabs. The Ulad Sulayman Arabs, who invaded their country from the north in the 1800s, were a long-standing enemy of the Tubu.

Today clan members are scattered in many different places, but they still consider themselves relatives. Members of the same clan usually help one another in cases of animal theft, which are still common today.

▼ CHIEFS ▼

In the past Tubu chiefs used to lead migrations and raids. The Tubu chief would decide when and where his people would move. In addition, the chief led raids on animals owned by neighboring groups. Only those with high status in society could take part in these activities. Chiefs were often chosen from among the most influential clan elders.

After colonization by the French in this part of Africa, chiefs had to be agreed upon by the colonial administration. Their main duty was to collect taxes for the French administration. This is still the case today, nearly forty years after independence. Besides this function, chiefs among the Teda and Daza enjoy very little power. The Tubu are very individualistic people, and every Teda or Daza man considers himself to be his own chief.

In Tibesti, the highlands where the Teda are found, there is a traditional chief called a *derde*.

This Tubu man from the Borkou region is cutting palm branches from a tree.

Tubu society does not fall under the authority of a main leader or leaders. Men are largely free to make their own decisions. Seen here is a meeting of men in Borkou.

This chief is chosen in turn from each of three leading families from the Tomagra clan. The Tubu in Tibesti nominated a new *derde*, named May Barkay, in November, 1996. This chief is supposed to decide conflicts and represent the whole community of Teda people in Tibesti. Today, the *derde*'s role is mainly symbolic.▲

chapter

7

MUSIC AND ART

THE TEDA AND DAZA PRODUCE AND LISTEN to the same kind of music. The Tubu society—in both Teda and Daza groups—has strict rules about singing and playing music.

While women, especially young women, may sing in public, they are forbidden to play any musical instruments. Men, on the other hand, can play musical instruments wherever they like. However, it would be shameful for a man to sing in front of an adult woman. Only the smiths can play a certain type of music with a drum.

Men, particularly the young, sing when they are far away from camps or villages. While they are riding alone or in small groups, men sing during their long camel treks across the desert. Filled with poetry and sadness, these songs are called "saddle songs."

The girls and young women sing a totally different type of music in the camps or villages.

While gathered in a circle, one girl leads the
song and the others answer in chorus. They
usually clap their hands and ululate. Sometimes,
they are accompanied by youths beating a large
drum, called a *nangara*. To its side, a smaller
drum called a *kwelli* may be beaten as well.

The smiths, the *aza*, are the only men for
whom it is not shameful to sing in public. A
smith is usually asked to come and play during
a celebration such as a wedding. He sings the
praises of the person or family who called for
him, hoping that they will reward him with
money for a good performance. The smith
accompanies the praise songs by playing his special drum, called a *kidi*. As he sings, young men
and women gather around him and dance in a
circle.

The Tubu also have two stringed instruments
that are played only by men. Though both
instruments look the same, they are played dif-
ferently. On one the strings are plucked like a
guitar. On the other they are played with a bow
like a violin. The body of both instruments is
made of wood or from an imported enameled
iron bowl. The body is then covered with dried
skin and a thin wooden neck is tied to the body.

The bowed instrument (or fiddle) has only
one string, and is played by the Teda of Tibesti.
The other type, with plucked strings (or lute), is
played by both the Teda and Daza. The Teda

The Tubu have rules about who may make particular kinds of music. Seen here is a smith playing the *kidi* for dancers.

AUTHORITY VS. CLEVERNESS

The Tubu, like most societies, use folktales to express moral values. The following Tubu tale was recorded in Niger in 1972. It contrasts the Tubu's approval of individual cleverness and initiative with their general dislike of authority and leaders. The contrasting qualities are symbolized on the one hand by the lion, representing powerful authority, and by the resourceful jackal on the other hand.

Lion and Jackal

Lion once told Jackal, "My bull just gave birth to a calf."

"You mean your cow, surely," said Jackal tactfully.

"My bull, I said," replied Lion arrogantly.

"But this is impossible," Jackal pointed out politely.

Lion was not used to anyone questioning anything he said. He immediately became hostile and adopted a threatening tone: "Are you implying that I'm *lying*?"

Jackal immediately realized it was pointless and probably dangerous to upset Lion any further. Since this route was leading nowhere, he hit upon another method of achieving his aim. He excused himself and saddled up a donkey. Leaping into the saddle, he rode toward Lion.

"Where are you going?" asked Lion.

"My father-in-law just had a baby, so I'm hurrying to visit him," said Jackal seriously.

"You must be joking! No male gives birth. Are you trying to make a fool of me?" said Lion.

"If a male does not give birth, why did you tell me that your bull had a calf?" replied Jackal.

play it with two strings, and the Daza often add a third, shorter string that produces a high-pitched sound.

The music played on these string instruments is said to speak, and listeners do recognize what it says. The musician, generally a young man, sometimes hums along. This music is rather sad and may seem repetitive when first heard; however, it has its own special charm and is full of subtle variety.

▼ OTHER ARTS ▼

The Teda and Daza have developed many folktales. These stories often mock authority and show a bitter sense of humor (*see box*).

The smiths make gold and silver jewelry, weapons decorated with simple designs, and leather crafts such as bags, shoes, and sheaths. On the whole, Tubu crafts are less complex than the famous Tuareg jewelry and leatherwork. The Tubu do not make sculpture.▲

chapter

8

THE FUTURE

THE FUTURE OF THE TEDA AND DAZA IS
closely related to the future of their country.
Today Chad is one of the poorest countries in
the world. This is partly due to the lack of natural resources in the region. The north is too
dry for agriculture, and only herders such as the
Tubu can live there.

Farmers in the south grow millet and a few
other crops for their own use, as well as cotton,
which is the most important cash crop. Except
for cotton processing there is almost no industry
in Chad. The country spends more money than
it earns and, without international aid, Chad
would be bankrupt.

The poverty of Chad has deep-rooted social,
historical, and political causes. The borders of
Chad, like those of most other African states,
were decided upon by colonial powers. These
borders are in many ways artificial, because they

do not contain people who are united as one society. One broad social split in Chad is between the north and south. The many different peoples of the south are primarily Christians or animists who live mainly from agriculture. The northern herders are Muslims who consider themselves to be superior to the farmers in the south.

After independence in 1960, the most highly educated people, who were settled people from the south, took leadership positions in Chad. Their abuse of power soon led the peoples from the north to revolt. This started a civil war that lasted for twenty years, from 1965 to 1985. The Teda and Daza played a leading role in this rebellion and a Tubu, Hissene Habre, became president of Chad in 1982.

He was not a good leader and was unable to solve the country's many problems. In 1990 he was overthrown by Idriss Deby, a man from the northeast, who is now president. Although the civil war ended over ten years ago, a great number of people still keep dangerous modern weapons such as machine guns, and many bandits roam the country. The 5 to 6 million inhabitants of Chad still lack electricity, running water, and modern roads, and there are few schools or medical facilities.

These services are especially hard to provide in the north, due to the great distances involved

The civil war in Chad between 1965 and 1985 had many negative effects. Many Tubu were killed. Others gave up their traditional way of life and moved into towns such as Faya Largean (above) for safety. But there was fighting in the towns too. Seen below is a street scene from Chad's capital, N'Djamena, in 1990.

and the very scattered and nomadic population. In the north children go to school only a few months a year, if at all. More than one child out of ten dies before puberty.

Many Teda and Daza men were killed during the civil war. This great loss has had lasting effects on the society. Many Tubu have given up their nomadic lifestyles and have settled in towns. But there is very little opportunity for employment and few of them have jobs. Poverty and the lack of outside aid mean that this situation is unlikely to change soon. As they have done in the past, most Tubu will probably continue to tend their herds to make a living.

However, rich mineral resources are known or suspected to exist in northern Chad. If the country is able to mine these resources some day, it would have enough money to make important improvements. Neighboring Niger has been able to improve conditions for its people by taking advantage of its mineral wealth. Many hope that Chad will be able to do the same thing.▲

Glossary

animist Someone who believes that natural phenomena and inanimate objects have souls.

aza The smiths, a subset of Tubu society.

caravan A train of pack animals and men that travel through the desert to trade goods.

derde A traditional chief whose role now is mainly symbolic.

dowry A gift the bride receives from her husband.

dromedary A camel with one hump.

kamaya Small farmer in Borkou and Tibesti.

kidi Long drum with two skins, played by the *aza*.

Koran Sacred book of the Muslims.

lute Musical instrument similar to a guitar.

maallem Muslim scholar.

malamala Large leather bag.

nangara Big Tubu drum.

shuwi Big calabash (gourd) used for churning milk.

Tu Local name for Tibesti, a highland region in northern Chad.

ululate Shrill sound of applause made by women.

yollumi Period following the wedding, when the young married couple has to live near the bride's parents.

For Further Reading

Most sources on the Tubu are written in French.
However, in English one can read the following:

Cline, W. *The Teda of Tibesti, Borkou and Kawar in
the Eastern Sahara, General Series in
Anthropology*. Menasha, WI: G. Banta
Publishing Co., 1950.
Nachtigal, G. *Sahara and Sudan*. Translated by
A. and M.J. Fisher. London: Hurst, 1971.

Challenging Reading

Baroin, Catherine. "The Position of Tubu
Women in Pastoral Production: Daza
Kesherda, Republic of Niger." *Ethnos*, Vols. 1
and 2, 1987, pp. 137–155.
Barth, Heinrich. *Travels and Discoveries in North
and Central Africa*. 3 vols. 1857. Reprint,
London: Frank Cuss, 1965.
Briggs, L.C. *Tribes of the Sahara*. Cambridge,
MA: Harvard University Press, 1960.
Clapperton, H. and D. Denham. *Narrative of
Travels and Discoveries in Northern and Central
Africa, in the Years 1822, 1823 and 1824*.
London: Darf Publishers Ltd., 1985.

Decalo, Samuel. *Historical Dictionary of Chad.* Metuchen, NJ: Scarecrow Press, 1987.

Martin, B.G. "Kanem, Bornu and Fazzan: Notes on the Political History of a Trade Route." *Journal of African History,* Vol. 10, No. 1, 1969, pp. 15–27.

Reyna, S.P. *Wars Without End: The Political Economy of a Precolonial African State.* Hanover and London: University Press of New England, for the University of New Hampshire, 1990.

For Listening

Chad: Music from Tibesti. Collection *Le Chant du Monde,* Harmonia Mundi, France, Compact disc LDX 274 722.

Index

ABOUT THE AUTHOR
Born in Paris, Catherine Baroin is a social anthropologist and researcher at the French National Center for Scientific Research. She received a Ph.D. in cultural anthropology from the University of Paris X–Nanterre. She has done extensive field research among the Tubu in the Republic of Niger and Chad and has published three books and many articles about the Tubu people.

PHOTO CREDITS: All photographs by Catherine Baroin, Ph.D.

CONSULTING EDITOR: Gary van Wyk, Ph.D.

LAYOUT AND DESIGN: Kim Sonsky